The Hummingbird's Tour

MARGARET DULANEY

The Hummingbird's Tour

Listen Well Publishing

Copyright © 2018 by Margaret Dulaney

All rights reserved. No part of this book may be reproduced in any form or by any electronic or mechanical means including information storage and retrieval systems, without the permission in writing from the author. The only exception is by a reviewer, who may quote short excerpts in a review.

Cover and interior design by Brooke Koven
Cover art and illustrations by Robin Phillips

ISBN 978-0-9986023-2-5

For more information about Margaret Dulaney, or to inquire about production rights, please visit

www.listenwell.org

HISTORY OF PRODUCTIONS

The Hummingbird's Tour received three developmental productions:

- ☞ The first in a private barn in Bucks County Pennsylvania in the Fall of 2013.
- ☞ The second at the Bucks County Playhouse in the spring of 2014.
- ☞ The third at the Theater at St. Clement's in New York City in the fall of 2015.

The play has yet to be reviewed at the time of publication.

The cast for all three productions was as follows…

Mattie: Susan Pellegrino
Norton: Ray Baker
Lucy: Anne O'Sullivan
Constance: Lynda Gravatt

The play was directed by **John Augustine**

CAST

The Siblings...

MATTIE: In her sixties. Fragile, energetic.
       The youngest of the siblings.

NORTON: Mattie's brother. The middle child.
       In his sixties. Bookish, a curmudgeon.

LUCY: Also in her sixties. The eldest.
       A free spirit, enthusiastic.

Their Caretaker

CONSTANCE: An African American woman in
       her eighties. Slow, grounded, dignified.

The time is the Spring of 1970.

The play

takes place in a comfortable, well lived-in living room/library in a house on a lake in northern California. There are tall, unorganized bookshelves lining the room with a makeshift ladder supporting a perch on top. One gets the impression that the room has been collecting books for the past thirty years or so, and the need for a ladder arose some twenty years ago, when the owner of the house commissioned a craftsman to build a structure in order for him to have access to the entire collection. Books spill out of the bookcase and gather around the room in book-puddles as well. A large picture window will be imagined downstage and facing the audience. There are two entrances: one leading to the hall / front door and bedrooms, and one to the kitchen / back door.

ACT ONE

• • • • • • • • • • • •

SCENE ONE

LIGHTS come up on the living room/library.

MATTIE comes racing out from the bedroom entrance and puffs over to the picture window, looks out for a second and disappears back into the hall. NORTON enters and moves up the library ladder and on to a perch at the top, takes a book, and sits. MATTIE races across stage and into the kitchen. MATTIE races back onstage and moves to the picture window, finally seeing someone through the glass, SHE gestures madly. Knowing SHE cannot be heard through the glass, SHE speaks under her breath, but distinctly so that her lips might be read.

MATTIE: Around the back!!
    (She gestures toward the kitchen)
      We'll surprise him!!
    (A little louder in her excitement)
      No idea you're coming!!

(She points to her head)
   No idea!!

(NORTON finally looks up from his book)

MATTIE: Around the back!!

(MATTIE runs into the kitchen)
(NORTON goes back to his book)
(SCREAMS of delight from the kitchen before MATTIE walks on carrying luggage, with LUCY following)

MATTIE: Now, where's our widower run off to? Never leaves his library, you know. A perfect fixture since the funeral. Oh, let's disguise you! We'll trick him! I've got just the thing!

(MATTIE tears off toward the bedrooms)
(LUCY moves over to the picture window and seems to study something)
(Pause)

NORTON: Greetings.

LUCY: Norton!

NORTON: So, the great avian sibling comes to roost.

LUCY: How long have you been up there?

NORTON: I'm always up here.

LUCY: Why didn't you say something?

NORTON: No one asked me anything.

LUCY: For goodness sake.

NORTON: I've observed something curious about our sister.

LUCY: What's that?

NORTON: It never occurs to her to raise her eyes above her own eye level.

LUCY: Is that right? An appropriate metaphor, don't you think?

NORTON: For?

LUCY: Well, her... her view of the world.

NORTON: If you mean in comparison to other more flighty outlooks, yes.

LUCY: Can't imagine whom you are referring to. Tweet, tweet.

NORTON: What gives us the pleasure?

LUCY: I was visiting an ashram and thought I'd swing by on my way home. Little surprise.

(NORTON looks confused)

NORTON: Swing by?

LUCY: Yes... Why are you making that face? ... Oh, no one goes to India anymore.

NORTON: They don't?

LUCY: It's nineteen-seventy.

NORTON: Oh, that explains it.

LUCY: It's less than an hour's drive from here. You were so smart to move to California.

NORTON: Place is lousy with ashrams, is it? And I always thought it was artichokes... Well, how was it?

LUCY: It was everything and more. You'd have hated it.

NORTON: Why is that?

LUCY: The creature would not have been comfortable.

NORTON: Hard beds?

LUCY: No beds at all.

NORTON: Good God, what possesses you?

LUCY: Man's search for meaning.

NORTON: Can't one search in comfort?
 Nice Lincoln Continental?

LUCY: That's a very good question, Norton. I don't know.

"Can't one search in comfort?
Nice Lincoln Continental"

NORTON: Well, I hope you found it.

LUCY: Found what?

NORTON: Whatever it was you were looking for.

    (Pause)

LUCY: It couldn't be a very flattering view from up there. I must look a sight from that angle.

NORTON: I like looking down on things.

LUCY: Yes... What were you reading, professor?

NORTON: Emerson.

LUCY: Does anyone read Emerson anymore?

NORTON: I believe a few still do, yes. My students often did, when forced.

LUCY: Hm.

NORTON: Let me guess. Outdated? Or is it that anything that smacks of the West these days is suspect. You'd rather I was reading one of your Eastern skimmers.

LUCY: Skimmers?

NORTON: Yes, you know the ones. Buddhism in twenty-five, easy-to-read, illustrated pages.

LUCY: I don't see why you moved to this state if you weren't going to take advantage of these things. Imagine Allen Watts as one's neighbor.

NORTON: Mr. Watts never sent over any cookies.

LUCY: There's a whole new way of thinking, Norton, practically at your doorstep and here you sit buried in the pages of a nineteenth century philosopher.

NORTON: You consider Buddhism to be a new way of thinking?

LUCY: Well.... Now, don't let's have an argument, professor, not in this stage of the game.

(MATTIE enters holding up a homemade bunny costume. SHE wears a headband with ears attached)

MATTIE: Ta da!

LUCY: Mattie.

MATTIE: Isn't it adorable?

LUCY: Did you mean for me to wear that?

MATTIE: Yes, you see, it just slips over whatever you're wearing.
(Pulling it over her clothes)
Snaps in the back. Lickety split. What do you think?
(Looks at Lucy's face)
We could pencil in your whiskers. It's really much more convincing with whiskers.

NORTON: You've been saving that one.

MATTIE: Norton! How long have you been up there?

NORTON: Half my life.

MATTIE: I never thought to look up.

NORTON: Exactly.

MATTIE: I feel such a fool.

NORTON: Can't imagine why.

LUCY: Why is it you have that, Mattie?

MATTIE: What?

NORTON: The get-up.

MATTIE: It's homemade.

LUCY: Well, yes.

NORTON: But, why?

MATTIE: To bring cheer. It's an Easter outfit.

NORTON: And who are the victims?

MATTIE: Victims?

NORTON: The unfortunates in need of cheering?

MATTIE: Out at the rest home.

NORTON: You mean to terrorize the old folks with that?

LUCY: She means to bring a little light to their lives on Easter. Don't you Mattie?

NORTON: God help me from ever living so long that a grown woman posing as a giant rabbit on Easter Sunday does anything but completely mystify me.

MATTIE: Norton, come down from there.

LUCY: He likes looking down on things.

NORTON: Like an angel.

LUCY: More like a panther.

NORTON: Like the angel of death, then.
    Lying in wait.

LUCY: Don't you think he has better things to do?

NORTON: Well, he has to be prepared at any moment, doesn't he, to drag us off to our appropriate destinations.

LUCY: Don't you imagine there's a specific date and time for that sort of thing? Couldn't he just read the list?

NORTON: So you think there's a knock-off calendar somewhere?

MATTIE: Oh Norton, really.

LUCY: To put it bluntly, yes.

NORTON: What an idea! And this appeals to your sense of... of what? of order?

LUCY: I guess you could say that.

NORTON: But you don't appear to like order. As far as I can see you live a life of complete chaos.

MATTIE: Complete chaos, Norton, really.

NORTON: There's a great gaping hole in this concept of yours. Do you see it?

LUCY: I've a feeling I'm about to have it pointed out to me.

NORTON: We can't get our hands on the information, you see. We'll never know whether that truck that ran us over have our name on it or was it simply a question of forgetting to look both ways.

LUCY: Let's say we did know? Knew the exact day?

NORTON: But we don't, do we?

(Pause)

MATTIE: So tell us about the nunnery, Lucy?

LUCY: Ashram.

NORTON: Yes, tell us. Did you find God?

LUCY: Wasn't looking for him.

NORTON: But did you find him?

LUCY: Norton, for the last time come down from that thing, would you?

NORTON: Give me one good reason.

LUCY: You can make us a drink.

(NORTON *heads down the ladder*)

MATTIE: At this hour?!

LUCY: Yes, we're celebrating.

MATTIE: I haven't had a drink in the middle of the afternoon in—

LUCY: The impulsive, Mattie! The impulsive is absolutely imperative in a woman of your age. If it doesn't come naturally, you must do your damndest to acquire it. Now where's Constance? She'll want to join us.

MATTIE: Constance won't drink on the job.

LUCY: You're not still pretending to employ her, are you?

(*Slight pause,* MATTIE *does not answer*)

NORTON: I'll get us some ice.

(HE exits toward the kitchen)

MATTIE: You know Constance is quite on her last leg, Lucy. Talks about it all the time.

LUCY: I've heard that before.

MATTIE: Yes, but she's serious this time.

LUCY: She's been on her last leg for over a decade, perfectly invincible, that leg of hers.

(CONSTANCE enters)

MATTIE: Yes, but this time one almost believes her. She's very grim.

LUCY: It's a great act. Trust me. Constance, like the cockroach, will outlive us all.

CONSTANCE: Lord have mercy.
 (Moving toward Lucy to get a close look)
 It's the other one.

LUCY: There she is, looking like the picture of youth. Aren't you happy to see me, Constance?

CONSTANCE: It's the three of you together, has me worried.

LUCY: We won't misbehave, I promise.

CONSTANCE: Hm.

LUCY: We're having a drink in the middle of the afternoon. Will you join us?

CONSTANCE: We'll need some ice.

LUCY: Norton's gone to get the ice. Sit down. You look as if you'd like to sit down.

CONSTANCE: Heading into the last turn, Lucy.

MATTIE: Constance, how dreary!

CONSTANCE: Neck-and-neck with the grave.

MATTIE: Really!

CONSTANCE: Stick around, could be a photo finish.

MATTIE: Now, that is the limit.

LUCY: Do you still hear the voices?

CONSTANCE: Loud and clear.

MATTIE: What voices?

"Neck-and-neck with the grave."

CONSTANCE: Dead people.

MATTIE: You don't tell me!

CONSTANCE: Whole damned choir of dead people.

MATTIE: I never heard about this.

CONSTANCE: Keep me up at night.

MATTIE: Are you sure it's not just the radio? Norton likes to play the radio at night.

(Pause as CONSTANCE focuses on Mattie's get-up)

CONSTANCE: What have you gone and done to yourself?

LUCY: It's her Easter outfit.

CONSTANCE: Is that it, huh. What's it supposed to be?

MATTIE: It's a bunny.

LUCY: It's for the old people.

CONSTANCE: Sweet Jesus! You going to wear that over to the home?!

MATTIE: Yes.

CONSTANCE: Easter Sunday?

MATTIE: I planned on it, yes.

CONSTANCE: Hm, mm, mm.

MATTIE: It's meant to cheer.

CONSTANCE: Is that it, huh?...
(SHE shakes her head)

Hm, hm, hm, hm, hm.
(NORTON enters with the ice)

NORTON: So what'll it be?

LUCY: Bourbon!

MATTIE: Bourbon! Good gracious! I could maybe handle a little sherry...

LUCY: Bourbon! It's derby day!

CONSTANCE: It's only the first of April.

LUCY: Ok, so, it's April fool's day, in the middle of the afternoon. I vote for bourbon!

NORTON: We might have some mint in the garden.

MATTIE: Juleps in April?! And it's still Lent!

NORTON: Don't tell me you gave up bourbon in the afternoon for Lent?

MATTIE: Well no, of course I—

LUCY: What did you give up, Mattie?

MATTIE: It's always so difficult to choose.

LUCY: Tell us.

CONSTANCE: Now, don't you go picking on the baby.

NORTON: Come on. Fess up.

CONSTANCE: She can give up fooling with the two of you.

LUCY: Tell us, Mattie, please. What have you given up?

(Pause)

MATTIE: Cocktail nuts.

NORTON: Good Lord!

MATTIE: Now Norton—

NORTON: The absurdities of that religion of yours!

MATTIE: It isn't just mine.

NORTON: Forty days and forty nights without cocktail nuts!

CONSTANCE: It'd be the death of me. I love cocktail nuts.

MATTIE: One has to make a stab at something.

CONSTANCE: I believe I know where there might be some mint. No bloodshed till I get back, hear.

(CONSTANCE exits)

MATTIE: Bourbon in the middle of the afternoon! What will become of us?

NORTON: Drunk will become of us.

MATTIE: There's something that's always confused me about drinking in the middle of the afternoon.

LUCY: What's that?

MATTIE: What does one do at cocktail hour?

NORTON: Well, there are a couple of ways you could go.

LUCY: Have you ever had too much to drink, Mattie?

MATTIE: Oh, not for years and years.

LUCY: Well it's something to work on then. Begin semi-annually and work your way up. Keeps one flexible.

MATTIE: I suppose you're right.

LUCY: I've always admired the professor's capacity for drink.

NORTON: Thank you.

MATTIE: Sometimes I wonder whether I've made a terrible mistake.

LUCY: What's that Mattie?

MATTIE: When I come to the end of my life, am I going to regret not having been more adventurous?

NORTON: Do you think you get extra points for adventurous?

MATTIE: Well, I don't know.

NORTON: You think when we get to the Pearly Gates, and there stands... Who is it stands at the gate, Mattie?

MATTIE: Peter! My word, Norton! Peter stands at the gate. You must remember that!

NORTON: Peter, then. Do you suppose Peter's going to be disappointed in our lack of daring?

MATTIE: Well, I hope not, because I would fail miserably.

NORTON: This is a ridiculous conversation.

LUCY: Don't tell me you don't think about these things, Norton.

NORTON: I'm here to think about life, not death.

LUCY: But death is a part of life.

NORTON: Yes, you know, I've heard that theory before. Bewildering. No, no, no. Life is life and death is death. That's why they have separate words for the things. We call them antonyms, I believe.

LUCY: Norton, this avoidance of anything worth discussing is really most annoying.

MATTIE: Seems to me, if you allow yourself to think about death every once in a while, it won't come as such a surprise.

LUCY: I find such thoughts to be vitally stimulating.

NORTON: Do you?

LUCY: Well, you know it's terribly important to Eastern thought. In the East they simply dwell on death.

NORTON: How cheery.

MATTIE: I hear Heaven's a lovely place.

NORTON: And, you heard this from whom?

LUCY: The greatest journey of them all, they say. Anyway, you can't get around the fact that there is a day with your name on it.

NORTON: The date of which I am blissfully ignorant.

LUCY: What if you were just handed the information? If, say, someone could tell you the exact date.

NORTON: Irrelevant.

LUCY: For discussion's sake, professor.

NORTON: I'd plug my ears and hum.

MATTIE: You wouldn't want to know?

NORTON: Would you?

MATTIE: Well, I really hadn't thought about it.

LUCY: Norton, don't tell me you wouldn't be curious.

NORTON: Not a bit.

LUCY: If someone could tell you...

NORTON: *(Plugging his ears)* Hum-dee-dumm-dumm.

LUCY: You're impossible.... Mattie would be curious, wouldn't you?

MATTIE: I'm not sure what I would be.

NORTON: A five-foot tall rabbit, by the looks of it.

(LUCY moves to the picture window)

LUCY: Well, I hope you two aren't going to be too much of a disappointment to me.

MATTIE: What?

LUCY: Just look at that view!

MATTIE: What were you saying, Lucy?

LUCY: Simply divine! It's no wonder you never leave your house, Norton. But then, you only left the house when Cynthia dragged you.

NORTON: Left to my own will, I prefer the sedentary.

LUCY: Well it's a splendid place to rot away, I must say.

MATTIE: Lucy!

NORTON: Solitude has never been high on Lucy's list.

LUCY: Well it might have been but... how does one meet people?

NORTON: Perfect.

LUCY: I've met someone at the ashram.

MATTIE: Oh dear.

LUCY: No, nothing like that. I'm through with husbands. He's a young man. Too young even for me.

NORTON: That sounds familiar.

LUCY: He's a seer.

MATTIE: A what?

LUCY: A clairvoyant.

NORTON: Oh goody.
LUCY: You'd adore him, Mattie. He's just divine.

MATTIE: What's he apt to see?

LUCY: Oh, all sorts of things. He says he only has to look into your eyes and he knows all manner of things.

MATTIE: My word.

NORTON: What sorts of questions are liable to be asked of him, Lucy?

LUCY: The sky's the limit.

NORTON: An example.

LUCY: Well, suppose you were to ask... On what day am I to die?

MATTIE: Good gracious!!

NORTON: Lucy, you can't actually believe—

MATTIE: And he only has to look in your eyes?!!

(CONSTANCE enters with mint, singing "My Old Kentucky Home")

CONSTANCE: "Oh the sun shines bright on my old Kentucky home."

NORTON: Hogwash.

CONSTANCE: No it isn't either. Mint juleps. Middle of the afternoon. Not even Derby day...
(CONSTANCE moves over to the bar)

LUCY: You can think what you like, Norton.

NORTON: I've never needed permission for that.

CONSTANCE: Lord, that's the truth.

NORTON: You really buy all this mumbo jumbo, don't you?

LUCY: You might too if you met him.

NORTON: Pity you didn't bring the creature home with you.

LUCY: I did.

MATTIE & NORTON: What!?

LUCY: He's just down there by the lake. I asked him to give me half an hour to explain.

MATTIE: Lucy! How unnerving!

LUCY: You'll like him, Mattie. He's very unassuming.

CONSTANCE: Company?

NORTON: Company, Constance. I hope there's plenty of bourbon.

MATTIE: Do you think he's allowed to drink?

NORTON: I was more concerned about myself.

LUCY: Why would you ask that, Mattie?

MATTIE: Well, mightn't it cloud the... the...
(Waves her hands around)

CONSTANCE: AHHH!!

ALL THREE SIBLINGS: What?

CONSTANCE: We're all out of bourbon!

ALL THREE SIBLINGS: NO!

(Pause)

CONSTANCE: April fools.

ALL THREE SIBLINGS: Constance!

(CONSTANCE laughs while the others try and gather themselves.

(MATTIE moves to the window)

MATTIE: He doesn't look the type, really.

LUCY: What type?

MATTIE: Well, the... the type to...
 (Suddenly turning to Lucy)
 Tell me something, Lucy. He hasn't... told you?

LUCY: Told me what?

MATTIE: On what day you're to... to..?

LUCY: What if he has? Would you like to know?

MATTIE AND NORTON: *(Plug their ears and hum "My Old Kentucky Home")*
 Dum-dum-dum-dee dum, dum dum dum dee dum dum dum.

CONSTANCE: That's the spirit. Let's have us a julep.

MATTIE: *(Looking out the window)*
 He's getting up! He's standing up!

CONSTANCE: Hallelujah!

MATTIE: Pour us a quick one, Constance. I'm weak-kneed.

CONSTANCE: All that hopping you've been doing.

(MATTIE looks at her outfit)

MATTIE: Oh! Oh my goodness! I have to change!

NORTON: I don't see why. Hand me one too, Constance, I'm headed north.

(NORTON starts to head up to his perch)

LUCY: Norton, you're not going back up to your perch.

NORTON: That is exactly where I'm going.

MATTIE: Quickly Constance!

CONSTANCE: Never seen two people itch so for a drink.
(Handing Mattie a drink)
Now don't spill on the puppy.

MATTIE: Bunny!!!

NORTON: Constance, it's dry as a bone up here.

CONSTANCE: What has gotten in to you two? You'd think you'd been called to the judgment.

MATTIE: Well, I will not be called in a bunny suit!!

(MATTIE trots out toward the bedrooms)

CONSTANCE: *(Handing a drink to Norton)*
Here you go.

LUCY: Norton, you are not going to meet Peter from up there.

NORTON: Name's Peter, huh?

CONSTANCE: Wasn't that the name of that old dachshund of ours?

LUCY: The least you can do is meet the man eye-to-eye.

NORTON: That is exactly what I intend not to do. Cheers.

LUCY: So you don't think it's hogwash.

CONSTANCE: If this is hogwash, I'm one happy hog.

(The DOORBELL rings)

LUCY: I'll get it, Constance.

CONSTANCE: Constance hasn't answered the door since the fifties.

(LUCY *walks out toward the front door*)

MATTIE: *(Offstage)* Was that the doorbell?!

NORTON: "Never send to know for whom the bell tolls."

MATTIE: *(Offstage)* Oh, Norton, stop!!

NORTON: "It tolls for thee."

CONSTANCE: Something's going on around here.

(*MATTIE enters, having forgotten to remove her bunny ears. SHE smoothes down her dress*)

MATTIE: I must look a sight, mustn't I?

(LIGHTS OUT)

• END OF SCENE ONE •

ACT ONE

SCENE TWO

LIGHTS come up on MATTIE: and NORTON. It is two hours later. Mattie still wears her bunny ears.

MATTIE: That voice.

NORTON: Hm?

MATTIE: That voice of his.

NORTON: Didn't notice his voice.

MATTIE: You didn't? Eerie.

NORTON: Couldn't get past the handshake?

MATTIE: Handshake?

NORTON: Don't tell me you didn't notice the handshake.

MATTIE: Odd what one first notices.
   (Pause)
   It was nice of him to offer to cook us dinner.

NORTON: Nice?

MATTIE: Well, don't you think? The first night?

NORTON: Presumptuous.

MATTIE: Didn't think of it that way. I wonder how Constance is taking it.

NORTON: Constance hasn't cooked dinner for decades.

MATTIE: Yes, but she's particular about the kitchen. I'm almost afraid to go in there... Could you meet his eyes, Norton?

NORTON: Can't remember.

MATTIE: Oh, you're impossible, of course you remember. I must admit I did everything in my power to avoid it. She did say it only took one look.

NORTON: Mattie, you can't seriously believe the little humbug has powers.

MATTIE: Well, I—

NORTON: The things that sister of ours will fall for. Staggering!

MATTIE: So you think he's an imposter.

NORTON: Complete phony!

MATTIE: Where does she get this from?

NORTON: First born. She inherited all of the dominant sucker genes. We'll be entertaining the Ragavad Neesh Neesh next.

MATTIE: Who?

NORTON: Oh just another cake mix to enlightenment, loaded with strychnine of course. There's a whole passel of dupes in this country. They claim the church's dogma is crushing them as they dance in the arms of some crackpot guru with a list of laws as long as the Nile. Those who are eligible should run off to Canada like sensible draft dodgers, but not our Lucy, no… No, if they'll have her, she'll be had.

(LUCY enters from the kitchen. SHE absently holds the door open for a moment, allowing an OTHERWORLDLY LIGHT to emanate from the kitchen. The LIGHT is accompanied by soft, heavenly MUSIC. All THREE onstage fall into a dreamy,

euphoric state for a moment before LUCY closes the door, shutting out the MUSIC and LIGHTS. THOSE ONSTAGE snap out of their reverie)

LUCY: Well, what do you think?

MATTIE: Lucy, you haven't left the boy alone in there with Constance.

LUCY: That's exactly what I've done.

MATTIE: But you know how Constance feels about the kitchen.

LUCY: They're getting on famously. You really must try and trust that people know how to communicate, Mattie. This isn't football. We don't need men in stripes, blowing whistles. Now you must promise to leave them alone. I'm going to knock the dust off.

(LUCY exits toward the bedrooms)

MATTIE: Norton, you have to go in there.

NORTON: But we promised.

MATTIE: We did nothing of the kind.

NORTON: Don't worry, Constance could flatten that

kid in one round. No question. You saw that physique of his.

MATTIE: Physique?

NORTON: Constance could snap him like a potato chip.

MATTIE: Are we talking about the same person?

NORTON: Worry about the boy, not Constance.

(Pause)

MATTIE: I have to admit, I was almost a little disappointed.

NORTON: Disappointed?

MATTIE: Yes. That voice.

NORTON: What voice?

MATTIE: Don't tell me you didn't notice his voice!

NORTON: You mean you wanted him to be genuine?

MATTIE: Well no. No, of course, I... No! ... Although it might be freeing.

NORTON: To know when you're to die?

MATTIE: Well, to… to know a little of the future. It might be… liberating.

NORTON: Not sure your church would approve of that.

MATTIE: My church wouldn't have to know.

NORTON: Don't tell me you'd sell your faith for a glimpse of the future.

MATTIE: I never knew you put any stock in my faith.

NORTON: Faith is something that can be relied upon in others. Like knowing you have a copilot aboard. It's reassuring.

MATTIE: Aren't you at all curious to know what's coming?

NORTON: Good Lord no. And I don't read the ends of novels before I've finished them.

MATTIE: I do.

NORTON: Mattie!

MATTIE: Well, I want to be prepared if the thing ends unhappily.

NORTON: I'm amazed at you!

MATTIE: You've never been tempted to skip forward? See what you're in for?

NORTON: Wouldn't dream of it. This is shocking behavior.

MATTIE: Well... Takes all kinds, you know... Variety.

NORTON: You refer to the difference between you and me.

MATTIE: Yes. Variety. So dull without it.

NORTON: Does this mean you don't wish to continue this conversation?

MATTIE: No, no. Not at all.

NORTON: Good, because I was just about to draw an interesting conclusion.

MATTIE: Oh goody.

NORTON: Just a theory.

MATTIE: Well, let's have it.

NORTON: Seems to me you've spent most of your life preparing for an unhappy ending.

MATTIE: Good heavens! Norton! Do you really think that?!

NORTON: Well, I—

MATTIE: What a dismal idea!

NORTON: Isn't that what your religion is all about?

MATTIE: It is not just my religion.

NORTON: Well, it's certainly not mine.

MATTIE: You think I go to church because I fear an unhappy ending?!

NORTON: In a sense, yes.

MATTIE: Well, there's no reasoning with you then, is there?

NORTON: Why not try? We could have a healthy philosophical argument. It goes well with bourbon in the afternoon.

MATTIE: Only the very coarse defend their faith. It's unattractive.

NORTON: Well, if you won't defend your faith, the least

you can do is confess to your fears. What is it you fear about the future?

MATTIE: Wasn't aware that I did fear the future.

NORTON: Put it this way, what is your idea of an unhappy ending?

MATTIE: You mean in a novel?

NORTON: That'll do. Give me an example of an unhappy ending?

MATTIE: Well, you know... When everyone dies in the end.

NORTON: But everyone does die in the end!

MATTIE: You said we were discussing novels! Don't get tricky on me, Norton. I've had far too much bourbon.

NORTON: Why this recent fascination with the old folks, Mattie? What's that all about?

MATTIE: I thought I should volunteer.

NORTON: That doesn't answer the question.

MATTIE: I thought I might cheer them up.

NORTON: Exactly. So you find them sad. Because it's an unhappy ending.

MATTIE: Norton, you're growing irritating.

NORTON: And why do you continue to employ Constance when she hasn't worked for fifteen years? Because you couldn't bear the unhappy ending.

MATTIE: Constance is part of the family!

NORTON: Yes, but not every member of the family draws a weekly salary for doing nothing.

MATTIE: You don't want Constance to leave, do you?

NORTON: Of course not. Just trying to have a discussion with a little depth.

MATTIE: But these are my depths, Norton, and I think I have a right to remain in the shallows.

NORTON: All right, I'll be quiet.

MATTIE: Can't think what's possessed you.

NORTON: I'm sorry, Mattie.

MATTIE: And, Constance stays!!

(LUCY reenters from the bedrooms)

LUCY: What on earth is going on in here?

NORTON: We were trying to have an argument.

LUCY: Splendid idea. I'll leave you to it.

MATTIE: Lucy, please send Constance out here, won't you? I'm sure she's exhausted.

LUCY: Exhausted is something you can pretty much bank on in Constance.

(CONSTANCE enters from the kitchen. The same effect of LIGHTS and MUSIC stuns ALL FOUR for a moment, as Constance holds the door open. LIGHT and SOUND shut off when the door shuts)

CONSTANCE: Shoowee!

LUCY: There she is, looking fresh as rain.

CONSTANCE: Lord have mercy.

LUCY: You haven't left Peter entirely alone in there, have you?

MATTIE: Does he have a last name?

LUCY: Hm?

MATTIE: This Peter. Was he given a last name?

LUCY: I really don't know.

MATTIE: Really, this new generation...

LUCY: Mattie, be careful. Your fuddy duddy's showing.

(LUCY holds the kitchen door open a second or two, allowing for a brief touch of LIGHTS and MUSIC. CONSTANCE, MATTIE: and NORTON swoon slightly before LUCY exits, shutting the door behind her. LIGHTS and MUSIC out)

MATTIE: What do you have to report from the kitchen, Constance?

CONSTANCE: That is some piece of business in there. Let me tell you.

NORTON: You are referring to the great mystic.

CONSTANCE: Bunch of hoo-doo, voodoo. Your sister

in there just sucking it down like moonshine. Hanging on every flimmy flam word. Sweet Jesus, that woman would buy doggy-doo if the right person was selling it.

MATTIE: But she believes the poor creature has powers.

CONSTANCE: Power to irritate. Messing around in that kitchen like he lives here. "You don't need to tell me where things are," he says, "I'll know." Leaving the refrigerator wide—

MATTIE: Did he know?

CONSTANCE: Hm?

MATTIE: Did he know where things were?

CONSTANCE: Doesn't take a wizard to know pots on the bottom plates on the top. You've seen that nose of his.

NORTON: Nose?

CONSTANCE: Fellow could track down a spice rack if it was buried in the basement.

MATTIE: I didn't notice his nose.

CONSTANCE: Nose like a front porch. Sniffing

through everybody's business. Messing with people's minds.

MATTIE: What's he saying?

CONSTANCE: All sorts of mole trap about uprisings and revolutions.

NORTON: Good Lord.

CONSTANCE: Namibia, Angola, South Africa—

MATTIE: Constance! How disquieting!

CONSTANCE: My people all around the world, blood mixing with all blood. My people in every house, the White House.

NORTON and MATTIE: The White House?

(Pause as THEY absorb this, smiling dreamily)

MATTIE: Still… We have to do something.

NORTON: What do you propose we do?

MATTIE: Someone should speak to Lucy.

NORTON: Have you ever gotten between Lucy and one of her charlatans?

MATTIE: Well.

NORTON: Remember the Yogi?

CONSTANCE: Yogi the bear... And don't forget the panther.

MATTIE: Oh, Lucy's Black Panther.

CONSTANCE: Him and that nasty head of hair.

MATTIE: Someone should try and reason with her.

NORTON: Never been known to work before.

CONSTANCE: In there giving everybody the heebie-jeebies.

MATTIE: You see how he's upset Constance?

CONSTANCE: Don't you worry about Constance. Constance got his number. Yessir. Called him on his two-headed hokey-poky.

NORTON: What did I tell you, Mattie. Fellow doesn't stand a chance against Constance.

MATTIE: Well, tell us.

CONSTANCE: After Lucy stepped out of the kitchen

he turns around and gives me one of those beady looks, like he's figuring on reaching down, grabbing something out of my stomach.

MATTIE: Constance!

CONSTANCE: Squints his little fish eyes at me and says—

NORTON: Fish...?

CONSTANCE: ...And says... "April 14, 1 pm."

MATTIE: What?!

CONSTANCE: April 14, 1 pm.

MATTIE: Constance! ... He didn't give you a year?

CONSTANCE: Didn't have to.

MATTIE: Oh dear.

CONSTANCE: He was so off to begin with... So I said, "wrong, Mr. Socrates, you're just as wrong as you look. I was born October 18, 8 am. Eighteen-and-eighty-eight. My Mama wouldn't lie about a thing like that."

MATTIE: April 14th. That's Easter Sunday. That's in two weeks.

CONSTANCE: Well, happy un-birthday to me.

(Pause)

NORTON: Well.... Maybe he plans on staying with us that long. Could be a portent of when we're finally shed of the fellow.

CONSTANCE: Sweet Jesus, I'll be stretched out in the grave by then.

MATTIE: Constance!

CONSTANCE: April 14, 1 pm. Bunch of juju jitzu—

MATTIE: Norton, something has to be done. You must speak to him directly.

NORTON: What an unpleasant idea.

MATTIE: He must be asked to leave. Politely, of course.

NORTON: How does one do that politely?

MATTIE: We can't have the creature hanging around inspecting our stomachs. I won't be able to eat a thing.

CONSTANCE: Dinner with Medusa.

MATTIE: Really, this is exasperating!

NORTON: So you think I should march into the kitchen and ask the fellow to pack it in?

MATTIE: Better to pack it in before he unpacks.

CONSTANCE: Nothing to unpack.

MATTIE: What?

CONSTANCE: You seen any luggage?

MATTIE: Well, that makes it easier.

NORTON: You really want me to ask him to leave, Mattie?

MATTIE: We can't have him pointing fingers and throwing out dates. It's highly unsettling.

NORTON: You're really serious about this.

MATTIE: That aggravating stare of his. As if one had two heads.
(SHE touches her head and discovers her bunny ears)
    AHHH!
(Ripping the bunny ears off her head)
    How could you have let me meet the boy with bunny ears on?!! NORTON!!!
    How humiliating!! REALLY!!... Well, you must ask him to leave immediately. That's all there is to it.

NORTON: Because he's seen you in bunny ears?

MATTIE: Because he's stirring things up! I do not like things stirred up!

NORTON: Mattie this is unlike you.

MATTIE: He could be anyone. Lunatic!

NORTON: I'm sure he is, but Lucy's funny about her lunatics.

MATTIE: She'll thank us for this later.

NORTON: Well, I'll tell you what I will do, I'll slide into the kitchen, have a look.

MATTIE: Send Lucy on an errand of some sort. Have a word with him alone.

NORTON: I'll see what I can do.
>   *(NORTON walks through the kitchen door allowing a slight hint of SOUND and LIGHT to seep through. MATTIE and CONSTANCE react, the door shuts and THEY snap back to reality)*

MATTIE: Simply infuriating, these types.

CONSTANCE: Mm, mm, mm.

MATTIE: Hanger's on.

CONSTANCE: Mm, hm.

MATTIE: There are some people that just don't belong.

CONSTANCE: Hm.

MATTIE: You mustn't dwell on any of this, Constance.

CONSTANCE: Any of what?

MATTIE: Dates and Predictions. That sort of nonsense.

CONSTANCE: Who do you think you're talking to?

MATTIE: But even if you don't believe a word, it can toy with your head.

CONSTANCE: Don't you go worrying about this old head.

MATTIE: Just so I know you haven't taken any of it to heart.

CONSTANCE: What has gotten into you?!

MATTIE: Bourbon, for one thing, and aggravation.

Really, Lucy does play the most annoying tricks. Such a nuisance!

CONSTANCE: You'd think you'd be used to it by now.

MATTIE: What?

CONSTANCE: Lucy's been messing with you ever since you were born.

MATTIE: Has she, Constance?

CONSTANCE: You don't remember?

MATTIE: I was a child.

(LUCY enters from the kitchen, with just a touch of SOUND and LIGHT. MATTIE and CONSTANCE react slightly and snap back)

LUCY: Well, I am getting quite an education, I can tell you.

MATTIE: Lucy, you don't really believe—

LUCY: The man is a genius.

CONSTANCE: Genie.

LUCY: Perfectly fascinating. Just heaps of information!

MATTIE: But, you can't honestly—

LUCY: Mattie? Where are your ears?

MATTIE: Really! How could you have let me?—

LUCY: Peter was absolutely charmed. Went on and on about you.

MATTIE: What?

LUCY: Couldn't take his eyes off of you. Said you appeared to glow.

MATTIE: Glow?

LUCY: I suppose it's all those years in that church of yours.

MATTIE: It really isn't just my—

LUCY: Said you were very highly evolved. Just streets beyond the rest of us.

MATTIE: Really?

LUCY: Claimed you were just filled with all sorts of lovely light.

MATTIE: Is that right?

LUCY: Couldn't say enough about you. Can't wait to get to know you better.

CONSTANCE: Well get on in there, Judas.

LUCY: And Constance! My goodness what a hit you've made!

CONSTANCE: Constance?

LUCY: You've a friend for life, I can tell you that.

CONSTANCE: Well, I'll be damned.

LUCY: And, look at these? Such fun.
   (SHE pulls four envelopes from her pocket)
   Four envelopes, each with our names on them. Some sort of marvelous mystical information inside, no doubt.

CONSTANCE: One with my name on it?

LUCY: Yes, but we're to save them for dessert. Specific orders. Mustn't cheat.

CONSTANCE: Let me see that?

LUCY: Now, Constance. You must promise me. No peeking.

CONSTANCE: Give it here.

(LUCY hands Constance the envelope)

MATTIE: Lucy, I'm sure the boy is gifted—

LUCY: Gifted! Mattie you are the master of understatement.

MATTIE: But don't you think you've gone rather overboard?

LUCY: That's my nature. You know that.

MATTIE: All that glitters, Lucy—

LUCY: This one is pure gold, you can trust me. Well, you saw those eyes.

MATTIE: Eyes?

LUCY: Don't tell me you didn't notice his eyes?

CONSTANCE: Have to look past the nose first.

LUCY: Nose?

CONSTANCE: *(Turning the envelope over)* This thing's about to burn little holes through my fingers.

LUCY: Constance, behave yourself.

(LUCY sees something out the picture window)

LUCY: Is that Peter out there? What on earth is he doing?

(NORTON enters from the kitchen, holding the door open for a moment. This time there is no Light or Sound)

LUCY: Norton, what is Peter doing outside? It's nearly dark.

NORTON: Had a word with the fellow.

LUCY: A word?

NORTON: Well, several words, really. Whole sentences to be exact. If I remember correctly, his last complete sentence went something like this—"Would you be happier if I just disappeared?"

LUCY: What?!

NORTON: And I had to admit I would.

LUCY: Norton!

NORTON: And so he pushed through the back door with that little step of his.

LUCY: He didn't really promise to disappear, did he?

NORTON: I quote him exactly.

MATTIE: Look, he's waving! What shall we do?!

(THE THREE SIBLINGS wave)

(CONSTANCE rips open her envelope)

CONSTANCE: Will you look at this?

(THEY all turn to look at Constance)

LUCY: Constance!

CONSTANCE: Well, happy Easter to you too, Mr. Socrates.

(All FOUR of them look back out and suddenly go into various stages of complete shock)

(LIGHTS OUT)

• END OF SCENE TWO •

ACT ONE

● ● ● ● ● ● ● ● ● ● ● ● ●

SCENE THREE

LIGHTS up on the THREE SIBLINGS sitting in a daze, staring out into space. It is three hours later that same night.

MATTIE: Poof.

LUCY: Mm?

MATTIE: Poof. Just like that.

LUCY: Mm.

    (Pause)

NORTON: I'm going back out there.

    (NORTON stands)

LUCY: Norton, you've been over the spot five times. There's nowhere he could have gone.

(NORTON sits)

MATTIE: Poof.

NORTON: A grown man doesn't just disappear.

MATTIE: Like a mole down a little hole.

NORTON: He did sort of favor the mole, didn't he?

MATTIE: Mole?

NORTON: Well, that face.

LUCY: Face?

MATTIE: Mole?

NORTON: A grown man doesn't just disappear.

(Pause)

MATTIE: Poor Constance.

LUCY: Could hardly speak.

NORTON: Hair stood on end.

MATTIE: Poor Constance... I hope she's able to sleep.

LUCY: That woman would sleep through a world war in her back yard.

MATTIE: April fourteenth.

LUCY: She hasn't a clue what it means.

MATTIE: Praise heaven for that.

"That woman would sleep through a world war in her back yard."

LUCY: I suggest it stays that way.

MATTIE: Good gracious! None of us would tell her!

(NORTON stands)

LUCY: Norton?

NORTON: I'm going back out there.

LUCY: What can you possibly hope to find?!

(NORTON sits back down)

(Pause)

(MATTIE notices the envelopes)

MATTIE: *(Gasps)* Oh!

LUCY: What is it?

MATTIE: *(Pointing at one of the envelopes)* My name! How did he know my given name?!

LUCY: I might have told him.

MATTIE: Did you?

LUCY: Can't imagine why I would have. Never use it myself.

MATTIE: Spooky.

NORTON: Congratulations Mattie. You have finally mastered the obvious.

MATTIE: Don't tease me when my nerves are on end.

LUCY: How can you two bicker at a time like this? Perfectly childish.

NORTON: Oh, pardon us Pope Pious.

LUCY: The point is what are we to do?

MATTIE: Not a thing at the moment. Our heads are entirely too muddled.

LUCY: We'll wait until morning, then.

NORTON: What do you think another day will bring?

MATTIE: A little distance.

NORTON: There's only one thing we can do to give us distance from those envelopes.

MATTIE: What's that?

NORTON: Throw them away.

MATTIE: Norton!

NORTON: Well, it's an option.

LUCY: We might kick ourselves later.

MATTIE: Then he hadn't told you?

LUCY: I've no idea what's inside that envelope.

NORTON: All in the same boat, eh? Then we really could destroy them, keep on as we have been.

LUCY: Sounds rather dull.

MATTIE: Think of the enormous change it would make if we opened them.

LUCY: Cataclysmic.

MATTIE: But perhaps we're meant to change.

NORTON: Change is for mid-life.

MATTIE: Grow then.

NORTON: Growth is for teenagers.

MATTIE: Well, we still aren't absolutely positive... How can we be sure there's any truth to them?

LUCY: You don't think the boy's disappearing in front of our very eyes?...

NORTON: Does add considerable weight to the damned things, doesn't it.

MATTIE: We really won't be absolutely sure until...

NORTON: Until?

LUCY: Well, you know.

NORTON: Easter Sunday?

LUCY: Perhaps we should postpone? At least until... until Easter. Until we know.

NORTON: It's a thought.

MATTIE: Two entire weeks!

NORTON: But nothing's really changed. We'll push on just have we have been.

MATTIE: Just as we have been, yes...

(pause as she stares at the envelopes)
There must be a reason why we're not meant to know these things. Don't you think?

LUCY: Well, for that matter, there must be a reason for the visit, the envelopes.

NORTON: There must be a reason. There must be a reason. A highly abused phrase. Why must there be a reason?

(Pause as THE WOMEN look at him blankly)

NORTON: We should make a pact.

LUCY: What sort of pact?

NORTON: It's all or nothing. No secrets from each other. They should be either open to the public or closed to us all, forever.

MATTIE: Good gracious!!

LUCY: What is it Mattie?!

MATTIE: Well, I hadn't thought of seeing the other two. Mercy!

LUCY: You don't like the idea of sharing?

MATTIE: It will make it infinitely more difficult. Don't you think?

LUCY: Yes, I do think.

NORTON: Well, we have two weeks to think. I suggest we go to bed.

MATTIE: It is getting late.

NORTON: I might just take one more look around outside before I turn in.

(NORTON stands)

LUCY: Norton!

(NORTON sits)

MATTIE: We'll all be brighter by the light of day.

(MATTIE stands to leave)

NORTON: Well.
(Standing to leave)
I can carry on with my inspection in the morning.

(NORTON and MATTIE work their way toward the bedrooms)

MATTIE: Lucy?

NORTON: You're not coming?

LUCY: Yes. Yes.

> *(LUCY rises and moves toward the door)*
>
> *(MATTIE and NORTON exit)*
>
> *(LUCY switches off a wall switch LIGHT, plunging the room into near-darkness)*
>
> *(LUCY lingers, gazing at the envelopes, which seem to glow faintly in the dim LIGHT. She moves nearer, and the LIGHT on the envelopes grows brighter and brighter, as crickets and the SOUNDS of the night swell outside)*

(LIGHTS OUT)

• END OF ACT ONE •

ACT TWO

SCENE ONE

LIGHTS come up on MATTIE, in a bathrobe, at the picture window. SHE is holding a cup of coffee and watching Norton as he hunts around outside. It is the next morning. The envelopes are in their place, but slightly askew. Again, MATTIE'S conversation is in half whispers and large gestures.

MATTIE: Really, Norton! Come in this minute! Where are your shoes for goodness sakes?!..
(Losing her connection with him)
Has to be the most stubborn...
(Catching his eyes again)
I'm having coffee!!
(She takes a big whiff of her coffee and loses the connection again)
Why, why, why, why, why is the man such a donkey? Out there in nothing but his pajamas. It's indecent.
(Catching his eyes again)

Found any trap doors? Any screens?! Now come in this minute before someone sees you!!

(LUCY enters)

LUCY: Don't tell me he's out there already.

MATTIE: Have you ever?..

LUCY: Well it's gotten him out of the house.

MATTIE: You think it's my fault he doesn't go out much?

LUCY: Why do you ask that?

MATTIE: Well, since Constance and I moved in, he's hardly budged.

LUCY: I saw how helpless he was after Cynthia died.

MATTIE: I'm overly sensitive, you know.

LUCY: To what?

MATTIE: The unhappy ending.

LUCY: Norton had such a clear shot at the happily ever after, didn't he, poor thing... Do you think this is really harder in a way on him than on us?

MATTIE: What do you mean?

LUCY: Last night. The disappearance. He's such a realist. You and I aren't so thrown by this sort of thing, but Norton... Norton has spent most of his life trying to disprove the miracle, hasn't he?

MATTIE: Well.

LUCY: Well?

MATTIE: Well, I'm not so sure about the miracle, myself.

LUCY: Not so sure?

MATTIE: I'm not so sure I approve, really.

LUCY: Of the miracle?

MATTIE: Miracles are really more for Catholics, those types.

LUCY: Mattie!

MATTIE: Garish. We don't talk of them much.

LUCY: But the bible is spilling over with the things!

MATTIE: Well, yes but... That was then.

LUCY: Really, the church has gotten so watered-down. I wonder you don't get wildly bored with it.

MATTIE: Lucy!

LUCY: No amount of guitar masses is going to save a dying ritual.

MATTIE: I don't think I can listen to this.

LUCY: Where's the magic?

MATTIE: Magic is for sorcerers.

LUCY: Then, show me where the sorcerers go to church, sounds loads more fun.

MATTIE: Oh Lucy…

LUCY: There's a whole new age upon us, Mattie, where all of the major religions are being melted down into one lovely sort of soup of faith, one marvelous sort of medley of belief. The time is coming where you won't see the difference in them, Mattie. Mark my words.

MATTIE: I pray to God you are wrong!
(Pause)
    Well… Variety.

LUCY: Variety?

MATTIE: Takes all kinds.

LUCY: What are you talking about?

MATTIE: Just imagine the world if we all thought the same.

LUCY: Horrible.

(MATTIE looks back out the window)

MATTIE: Norton, is this really necessary?! Get back in here this minute!

LUCY: Yes, come and join us, professor! We're having a lovely chat about religion. You can sharpen your claws!

MATTIE: How could we have turned out so differently?

LUCY: We've always been different.

MATTIE: Yes but, how does this happen? The same parents, the same upbringing. Raised in the Episcopal church.

LUCY: Yawn.

MATTIE: And please no lectures on reincarnation.

LUCY: It's quite an ancient concept, Mattie, embraced by many of the world's religions. Really you Christians can be so near-sighted. You know, fully two thirds of the people on this planet are not in your camp at all.

MATTIE: Two thirds?

LUCY: Two thirds, non-Christian.

MATTIE: Not in the civilized world?!

LUCY: You are positively provincial!

(MATTIE looks back out the window)

MATTIE: What is the man up to now? As if the creature swam away in that chilly lake.

LUCY: You'd rather not discuss this, I take it.

MATTIE: I knew when that boy first walked in there'd be trouble. He's going to stir things up, I said to myself.

LUCY: Well maybe we need stirring.

MATTIE: I'm too old for stirring.

LUCY: You said last night perhaps we needed to change.

MATTIE: A day older a day wiser.

LUCY: If you're too old for a little stirring, then the date in that envelope of yours may as well be today.

MATTIE: Lucy!

LUCY: Well I hardly see the point.

MATTIE: I can't just live out the rest of my life as I am?

LUCY: You could, but where would be the interest?

MATTIE: You think I should run away with the circus?

LUCY: I suppose that was a reference to my life.

MATTIE: Well...

LUCY: If it makes you happy, yes.

MATTIE: I am happy.

LUCY: But you act as if it's all over. As if you're winding down. Both of you.

MATTIE: But that's what one does at this time of life.

LUCY: Oh Mattie, Mattie. This is the time you do all the things you've always wanted to do.

MATTIE: This is what I want to do.

LUCY: Volunteering at the rest home?

MATTIE: I thought I could bring them some life.

LUCY: Do you have any to spare?

MATTIE: Lucy!!.. I'm sure you didn't mean that. It's that creature! Those envelopes!

LUCY: They do shed a rather glaring light on things, don't they?

MATTIE: I've a good mind to throw them away. So disruptive!

(NORTON enters in pajamas and no shoes)

NORTON: What's disruptive?

MATTIE: This whole nasty experience. Those horrid envelopes!
(SHE walks over and picks up the envelopes)
I've a good mind to burn them.

NORTON: Remember our pact. Easter Sunday. You promised.

MATTIE: I did nothing of the kind.
(Looking down at the envelopes in her hands)
AHHHH!

LUCY: What is it?

MATTIE: They've been opened!

NORTON: Opened?!

MATTIE: Opened!

LUCY: All of them?

MATTIE: All of them.

NORTON: Who in the world...

LUCY: Opened and just slipped back in? No disguising?

MATTIE: Scotched taped!

NORTON: *(Turning to Lucy)* Well, isn't that interesting.

LUCY: Why are you looking at me that way, Norton? You can't possibly believe that I—

NORTON: Doesn't take much deducing. Mattie's genuinely shocked, I know I didn't do it, and Constance was in her nightly coma.

LUCY: I'm drawing a very different conclusion. Knowing that I did not open the things myself—

MATTIE: Horrible! To think that one of you knows my... my...

NORTON: Expiration date?

MATTIE: Odious phrase!

LUCY: Norton I will not have you looking at me that way.

NORTON: What way?

LUCY: As if you could see through my skin.

MATTIE: Now this has absolutely got to stop this minute!

LUCY: I know what you're trying to do, Norton. You used to do this to me as a child.

NORTON: And what is that?

LUCY: You're trying to discredit me.

NORTON: I used to do that to you as a child?

LUCY: Constantly.

NORTON: So I could see through you back them, could I?

LUCY: You were hateful. We couldn't have been more different.

MATTIE: Variety!

NORTON: Variety, yes. That means Mattie doesn't want to continue the conversation.

LUCY: Is that what that means.

NORTON: Yes, whenever you're having a difference of any kind, she sings out, "Variety". Sort of turns the issue around. Makes it a happy one.

LUCY: Spice of life, that sort of thing.

NORTON: That's it.

LUCY: Makes one wonder.

NORTON: What?

LUCY: Whether that cry of discovery was genuine.

MATTIE: You don't think that I—

LUCY: Well I'm not so sure.

MATTIE: Why would I do such a thing?

NORTON: You're the one who reads the ends of novels before you've finished.

LUCY: Mattie, you don't!

MATTIE: I like to be prepared!!!

NORTON: You see?

MATTIE: Now, stop it! Both of you! You're being horrid!

LUCY: You're being horrid!

NORTON: Little Mattie's battle cry!

LUCY & NORTON: You're being horrid!

(CONSTANCE enters)

CONSTANCE: What in the Devil's name is going on in here?

MATTIE: Now you see? You've woken Constance.

NORTON: We're trying to catch a rat-fink, Constance.

CONSTANCE: In here acting up like children.

MATTIE: Well, I'm going back to bed. Hardly slept a wink last night.

NORTON: It's no wonder.

LUCY: Up snooping around.

MATTIE: You're beasts! Both of you!

(MATTIE walks out toward her bedroom)

NORTON: Sneaky-peeker!

MATTIE: *(Offstage)* Monster heads!

CONSTANCE: Now you know better than to tease her like that.

LUCY: She gets away with murder with that phony innocence of hers.

NORTON: What are you complaining about? I was the one that always used to take the rap for her.

LUCY: I beg your pardon.

CONSTANCE: Lord, this is going to be long visit. How long you planning on stopping here, Lucy?

LUCY: Well, I have to... That is... At least… through... Easter.

CONSTANCE: Easter? Sweet Jesus!

NORTON: That is, unless there's an unexpected homicide.

CONSTANCE: You'd better go ahead and line up the squad car, then.

LUCY: Don't worry I've yet to stoop to manslaughter.

CONSTANCE: Line 'em up anyway.

NORTON: Here she goes.

LUCY: Why, Constance?

CONSTANCE: Trapped in here for two solid weeks with the three of you. Tell 'em bring along the paramedics.

LUCY: What for?

CONSTANCE: Couple of hefty ones.

LUCY: Why?

CONSTANCE: Come Easter Sunday, they'll have to drag me out of here in a body bag.

LUCY & NORTON: Constance!!

(Pause)

CONSTANCE: Norton why don't you run and put you some clothes on.

NORTON: These are clothes.

CONSTANCE: Running around dressed like a mental patient.

NORTON: They're pajamas.

CONSTANCE: You heard me.

(NORTON exits)

CONSTANCE: Lord, you can sure cause a commotion.

LUCY: Why do you blame it on me?

CONSTANCE: Don't you go messing with me, Miss Lucy. I knew you before you were born.
(Pause)

What you running from this time?

LUCY: I don't know what you mean.

CONSTANCE: Something's chasing you. I can see it in your eyes.

LUCY: I've come for a visit.

CONSTANCE: Hm mm.

LUCY: I was bored at home. I often get bored.

CONSTANCE: Hm mm.

LUCY: Must I always be running from something?

CONSTANCE: You tell me.

(Pause)

LUCY: Constance, these voices of yours?..

CONSTANCE: Hm mm?

LUCY: Are they any comfort to you?

CONSTANCE: What do I want with comfort?

LUCY: Everyone needs some comfort.

CONSTANCE: Something spooked you Lucy, I can see it as clear as my two feet. When you were little it seemed like something was always spooking you.

LUCY: Is that true?

CONSTANCE: Running from room to room, crawling in people's beds, your mama's bed, the other kid's beds, my bed. Spooked.

LUCY: I don't remember that.

CONSTANCE: Only difference is now you're running from state to state, husband to husband, guru to guru... What is it this time, Lucy?

(Pause)

LUCY: I came for a visit.

CONSTANCE: Hm mm... Now I want you to listen to what Constance has to tell you. Whatever it is making your hair stand up on end, you're going to have to face it one time or another. You keep running around looking for folks that are going to turn your life around. Turn your own self around and face it... Whatever it is... Face it... It'll back down.
(Pause)

LUCY: Have you ever been afraid of anything, Constance? You don't seem to fear anything, certainly not death.

CONSTANCE: I wouldn't say that. I fear death. Other people's death. Not my own. I feared my Mama's death. Thought it might drive me mad. It didn't. I feared one of you three might die when you were children. There were times when the chill of that thought threatened to drive me from my senses.
    You came close once and it almost ripped my head in two. But you lived, and I kept a hold of my mind. I've known fear. I know the way it smells... What's hunting you, Lucy?

(Pause)

LUCY: I came for a visit.

CONSTANCE: Hm mm...

(Pause. CONSTANCE stands)

CONSTANCE: And I'm Mary Poppins. I think I'll take a ride up the banister.

(CONSTANCE exits)

LIGHTS OUT
• END OF SCENE ONE •

ACT TWO

· · · · · · · · · · · · · · · · ·

SCENE TWO

LIGHTS come up on the empty room. It is morning one week later and the envelopes have not been touched. NORTON enters the room and walks over to the envelopes, pauses, reaches to touch them, pulls his hand away, reaches again, drums on the table with his fingers, hears something and scurries up his ladder. MATTIE enters, does not see Norton, freezes when SHE sees the envelopes, moves toward them and pauses, reaches toward them and pulls her hand away, crosses herself and races offstage.

LUCY: *(Offstage)* Morning!

MATTIE: *(Offstage)* Morning!

> (LUCY enters, stares at envelopes, turns to see if Mattie is out of sight, turns back to envelopes)
>
> (Pause)

NORTON: Morning!

LUCY: Norton! That ridiculous hiding place of yours!

NORTON: It's hardly very effective as that, is it? I'd have to choose some place very different to hide from you.

LUCY: And where might that be?

NORTON: Somewhere close to the ground.

LUCY: You really think I could blow away in a strong wind, don't you?

NORTON: Actually I consider you to be your own unique weather system, the kind that carries its own wind.

"I'd have to choose some place very different to hide from you"

LUCY: Hm... Well, one more week.

NORTON: That long? You promise to leave then?

LUCY: I've a plane reservation first thing Easter Monday.

NORTON: Well, that's good news.

LUCY: Lovely to feel so welcome.
(Pause)
At least I don't ruffle easily. Mattie seems completely undone by the whole affair. You know this is really hardest on her, don't you?

NORTON: What makes you think that?

LUCY: She's so rigid. That church of hers... We can bend with the kinks, accept the out of the ordinary, but Mattie's so... Well, she's just so entirely wedded to the ordinary, isn't she?.. Those envelopes...

NORTON: What about them?

LUCY: You'd think the devil himself was locked up inside.

NORTON: He isn't?

LUCY: You think this curiosity of mine very low, don't you, professor?

NORTON: It's your faith, worries me.

LUCY: I didn't think you gave a hoot about faith.

NORTON: We're all called upon to have faith. Lucy. Whether you put it in God or the Swiss frank, it's a fairly basic necessity. It's the ones that think they've cornered the market that are the dangerous ones.

LUCY: Well, that's one thing you can never accuse me of.

NORTON: No... Not you, no... You're on the hummingbird's tour of theology, aren't you?

LUCY: How's that?

NORTON: They only light for fifteen-second intervals.

LUCY: Hm... But this curiosity of mine is something you approve of.

NORTON: Curiosity is your greatest attribute, Lucy. It's what makes you almost tolerable.

LUCY: Why thank you.

"You're on a hummingbird's tour of theology aren't you?"

NORTON: And, if there is a life after this one, I don't imagine that all the words in this room could begin to describe it to us.

LUCY: I didn't think the faith of a realist dealt at all with the afterlife.

NORTON: Our minds can't be completely blank on the subject.

LUCY: So you think that you might see Cynthia again.

NORTON: Ah, I knew you'd find it.

LUCY: What?

NORTON: My Achilles' heel.

LUCY: The date in that envelope could be a very happy one for you. A long looked for reunion.

NORTON: It could.

LUCY: If only you believed.

(NORTON holds his foot out)

NORTON: Go ahead, give it another twist.

LUCY: I'm only trying to help.

NORTON: Is that what you're doing?

LUCY: Have you ever had any contact? ... with Cynthia? ... Since she died.

NORTON: Good lord, Lucy.

LUCY: Oh it's not such a bizarre notion. You wouldn't be the first mourner to mention strange occurrences, even complete visitations. You can't tell me you've never heard of such things...
 And you're about to say that nothing out of the ordinary has happened, not even a suggestion.

NORTON: Well, I ... Come to think of it, something did happen once.

LUCY: What?

NORTON: Damndest thing.

LUCY: Tell me.

NORTON: It was about a year after she died. Matter of fact, it could have been a year to the very day. I remember I went to bed early, couldn't have been more than eleven o'clock, I was sound asleep when something woke me.

LUCY: What?

NORTON: I'm not sure what it was exactly that brought me awake, whether it was the strange fragrance, or—

LUCY: What fragrance?

NORTON: Like roses.

LUCY: Oh, how glorious. Continue.

NORTON: As I was saying, I don't know whether it was the smell of roses or the sort of half-light of an opened door… or the shadow.

LUCY: Shadow?

NORTON: A shadowed figure at the foot of my bed.

LUCY: You don't tell me? What was it doing?

NORTON: It appeared to be holding something in its hand.

LUCY: What?

NORTON: I couldn't make it out exactly, but it was holding it up and slowly waving it over the bed, like this.

(NORTON waves his hand over his head slowly)

LUCY: Almost like a blessing of some sort.

NORTON: Yes, I suppose you could say that.

LUCY: Could you see the face?

NORTON: Not at first.

LUCY: What did you do?

NORTON: Well, I sat up in bed…

LUCY: And?

NORTON: Waited for my eyes to adjust.

LUCY: Well who was it?

NORTON: Constance, waving a can of air freshener. Said my room smelled of old books.

LUCY: Norton!!!

NORTON: Had you going, didn't I?

LUCY: You are positively loathsome!

(NORTON pretends to spray the room with air freshener)

NORTON: Pshhhh...

LUCY: You are ruthless! How did poor Cynthia put up with you?!

NORTON: I'd never have been able to pull something like that off on Cynthia. She could see through solids.

LUCY: Well, I miss her.

NORTON: Hm...
(Pause)

LUCY: Are you ever tempted to join her?

NORTON: Every day.

LUCY: You see? I knew you'd stopped living.

NORTON: It'll get easier.

LUCY: Not if you don't get out and—

NORTON: We all have different ways of licking our wounds, Lucy. My way wouldn't be your way.

LUCY: Variety?

NORTON: Exactly. And don't quote to me from one of your damned self-help manuals.

LUCY: Do I do that?

NORTON: You couldn't brush your teeth in the morning if some damned pop psychologist hadn't told you how to hold the brush.

LUCY: That's a slight exaggeration, don't you think?

NORTON: I actually find comfort in solitude, difficult as that may be to fathom, and I can safely say that I have never taken someone else's advice on how to live my life.

LUCY: Do you really think me that spineless, Norton?

NORTON: I simply cannot understand where you came from. Weren't we all brought up in the same house? By the same parents?

LUCY: Even puppies from the same litter will differ as dogs.

NORTON: Canines are trained.

LUCY: And we were not, thank God. If we were, where would we be now?

"Even puppies from the same litter will differ as dogs"

NORTON: We wouldn't be at odds.

LUCY: No we'd all be perfectly even and completely inflexible.

NORTON: Sounds like a winning personality to me.

    (MATTIE enters)

MATTIE: Well, I'm off to church. Anyone wish to join me?

NORTON: I will.

MATTIE & LUCY: Norton?!

NORTON: You see how shocking it would be if I changed? You depend on my stubbornness.

MATTIE: Is that what we do?

LUCY: I'll go with you, Mattie. I need a little airing and church should be just the thing, all that standing and kneeling, good for the spine. I'll be just a minute.

(LUCY exits)

MATTIE: You two aren't fighting again?

NORTON: Oh, Lucy's just getting a little restless. I imagine this is really hardest on her.

MATTIE: Why do you say that?

NORTON: Well, she has no mind of her own. No backbone. We at least retain something of ourselves when all goes haywire around us. Lucy completely falls apart.

MATTIE: Poor thing... Maybe it was all those husbands of hers.

NORTON: Each one ran off with a piece of her vertebra, you think.

MATTIE: Something like that.

NORTON: Hm.
 (Pause)

MATTIE: Why do you think I never married, Norton?

NORTON: You're just getting around to wondering that now?

MATTIE: Well, I'd left off wondering for years, but when one is faced with one's mortality...

NORTON: You thought you'd re-hash the issue, did you? Well, you certainly had lots of beaux.

MATTIE: Oh! What an old fashioned word.

NORTON: Would you rather I called them lovers?

MATTIE: Now don't be tacky.
 (Pause)
  Why did you marry?

NORTON: Because I was swept off my feet.

MATTIE: Sounds lovely.

NORTON: I can see no other reason to marry.

MATTIE: Never happened to me.

NORTON: Then, there's your answer.

MATTIE: Thank you, Norton. I knew you'd be able to help… I've been thinking.

NORTON: I can see that.

MATTIE: About Easter.

NORTON: What about Easter?

MATTIE: We must behave as if nothing's wrong.

NORTON: That'll be a first.

MATTIE: For Constance, you know. Now, I'm going to visit the home just as I planned.

NORTON: Not in that little cottontail number.

MATTIE: Easter Bunny! It's an Easter Bunny!… Please… I've been trying to work things out. What would you normally do on Easter?

NORTON: Easter… Let me think… Easter… hm… Haven't had a good egg hunt in years.

MATTIE: Norton, please.

NORTON: Easter falls on a Sunday this year, doesn't it?...

MATTIE: Of course, Easter!—

NORTON: Just trying to get all my bunnies in a row... Easter.. Easter Sunday...

(CONSTANCE enters)

CONSTANCE: What about Easter?

MATTIE: Oh, we... We were just—

NORTON: Constance should be able to help us out here. We were just trying to work out what a heathen does on Easter Sunday.

CONSTANCE: Isn't that when Lucy said she was fixing to leave?

NORTON: Thereabouts.

CONSTANCE: Well I know what I'll be doing.

MATTIE: What's that?

CONSTANCE: Taking that long stairway to heaven.

MATTIE: Constance.

CONSTANCE: You three have been messing with each other since you climbed out of the womb.

MATTIE: I don't remember it that way.

NORTON: Selective memory. That's what's so convenient about the past, isn't it? Now the future...

CONSTANCE: What about the future?

NORTON: Well, it seems to choose us, doesn't it?

CONSTANCE: If we're lucky.

MATTIE: Constance, really, you are too dismal these days. We're going to start calling you old Mrs. Doom.

CONSTANCE: Well, if this week's anything like this past one, with the three of you, you'd better find Old Mrs. Doom a nice big box.

NORTON: Here she goes again.

CONSTANCE: Line up the pallbearers.

MATTIE: Really.

CONSTANCE: Maybe I'll save you some trouble, slip into town this afternoon. Have myself embalmed.

MATTIE: Good gracious!

CONSTANCE: Better work on my funeral face, though, hadn't I? Don't want to go out looking like a stuffed fish... How's this?

(CONSTANCE lays her hands on her chest, closes her eyes and wears a placid smile)

MATTIE AND NORTON: Constance!!!

(LUCY enters wearing something very un-churchy)

MATTIE: Lucy, you're not going to church in that?!

LUCY: You think it will cause attention?

MATTIE: A silent uproar.

LUCY: Marvelous. Let's go.

(MATTIE and LUCY exit)

NORTON: There's something that confuses me Constance.

CONSTANCE: What's that?

NORTON: As far as I can tell, you've had one foot in the grave for thirty years.

CONSTANCE: Hm mm.

NORTON: What do you have to say about that?

CONSTANCE: Cold foot.

NORTON: Well, what prevents the rest of you from jumping in after it? What keeps you here?

CONSTANCE: Who else is going to take care of the three of you?

NORTON: We're in our sixties, Constance. We can feed and dress ourselves.

CONSTANCE: Hm mm.

NORTON: Well what if someone was to tell you that we'd get on just fine without you? What then?

CONSTANCE: Who's going to do that?

NORTON: Say it's one of those voices of yours.

CONSTANCE: Well, look who's talking voices.

NORTON: I shelve all skepticism for the sake of theoretical discussion.

CONSTANCE: Oh is that what you do, huh.... Something's eating you.

NORTON: I'm just trying to figure out what's keeping you here.

CONSTANCE: No you're not. You're trying to work out what it is keeping you here, Norton, and nobody can answer that question.
(Pause)
    Nobody can tell you that, nobody can tell you when it is you're going to see her again... You've

just got to figure on some day and some reason... You've just got to figure on living.

NORTON: Isn't that what I'm doing?

CONSTANCE: Poking around in this old library of yours, gathering dust.

NORTON: Not every widower bounces back like a bedspring.

CONSTANCE: I don't want you to bounce, Norton, just stand.

(Pause)

NORTON: Say someone could tell me that was I was going to see her again.

CONSTANCE: Who's that?

NORTON: Just say the information was available to me.

CONSTANCE: We're doing that again, are we?

NORTON: I wanted to go with her, Constance. I'd go this minute if the opportunity arose.

CONSTANCE: Lord you don't have to tell me that... And I wanted to go on with Mama thirty years ago. I've been prepared ever since to hop on any chariot that swung low enough.

NORTON: What keeps us here?

CONSTANCE: The reasons to stay are heavier than the reasons to go.

NORTON: That simple, huh?

CONSTANCE: Simple as that... When you were a child you were like rubber.

NORTON: Was I?

CONSTANCE: Bounce as high as the sky.

NORTON: Life was just a trampoline, was it?.. Afraid I've lost my bounce, Constance.

CONSTANCE: I don't want you to bounce Norton, just stand. When was the last time you took a walk?

NORTON: Walking is for Europeans.

CONSTANCE: You used to walk with Cynthia.

NORTON: She had some highfalutin, continental ideas about movement and sunshine. Look where it got her.

CONSTANCE: I'm talking about when she was alive, Norton. Cynthia lived while she was alive. Some people swear by that, you know, living. Some people say that's what we're meant to do with life. Live it.

NORTON: I'm living.

CONSTANCE: Like a mushroom, in here, feeding off old books and light bulbs.

NORTON: Give me time.

CONSTANCE: I don't have much of that left to give.

(Pause)

NORTON: Point taken.

CONSTANCE: Well, I think I'll tuck Constance in for her mid-morning nap.

(SHE picks up the newspaper and a pair of glasses)

(CONSTANCE exits)

NORTON: *(Pats his pockets and head, looking for his glasses)* Those were my glasses!

CONSTANCE: *(Offstage)* Hm mm.

(LIGHTS FADE)

• END OF SCENE TWO •

ACT TWO

· · · · · · · · · · · · · ·

SCENE THREE

It is morning, five days later, Good Friday. MATTIE and LUCY are discovered onstage when the LIGHTS rise.

MATTIE: Two more days.

LUCY: Then we get to open our little prizes, don't we?

MATTIE: You sound as if you're looking forward.

LUCY: Well it might clear up a few questions, mightn't it?

MATTIE: I don't see how.

LUCY: It will give us an idea of what might kill us, you see. If the date is thirty years from now, it's old age, if it's in three years, it's some horrible disease, and if it's next week, no doubt it's a truck or something of that nature.

MATTIE: What a gruesome imagination!

LUCY: I think all in all I'd like most to avoid the second one.

MATTIE: The horrible disease?

LUCY: That's the one. So you see we have a two to one chance of avoiding some horror.

MATTIE: I'm not sure how that makes me feel.

LUCY: Well, imagine the relief of turning up number one or number three.

MATTIE: You're not worried about anything, are you?

LUCY: What do you mean?

MATTIE: The horrible disease?

LUCY: Why do you ask?

MATTIE: Just seemed the natural conclusion.

LUCY: Well...

MATTIE: What, Lucy?

LUCY: Well, there is some question of a mysterious blob somewhere about the middle section.

MATTIE: Lucy. I had no idea.

LUCY: Actually, it's quite unfair to call it a blob. It really looks more like a rose, half opened.

MATTIE: What are you doing about it?

LUCY: Nothing.

MATTIE: You can't just do nothing.

LUCY: Lots of people do nothing about such things.

MATTIE: Not in the civilized world!

LUCY: Oh, there we go again with the civilized world. When I say I'm doing nothing, that really isn't the truth. I'm thinking an awful lot about it and it's most irksome.

MATTIE: What do you plan on doing?

LUCY: Nothing.

MATTIE: Lucy!.. Not even an alternative cure of some sort?

LUCY: Well, I might look into something like that, I'm really not sure yet. The truth is, I'm growing tired of seeking advice.

MATTIE: This is hardly the time to decide that!

LUCY: My life has belonged to so many different people. I'd like my death to belong to me.

MATTIE: You don't think you're dying, do you?!

LUCY: Well I'm not sure.

MATTIE: You don't feel ill, do you?

LUCY: Not at all, you see, that's the most absurd thing about your civilized world. I'm sure that roses bloom all the time inside of us, and like a rose naturally would, it drops its petals and nothing comes of it. But these modern types like to peer inside of us every quarter and see what's blooming. They scare us half to death and let our imaginations take care of the other half. The result, I'm afraid, is just what you went to them to prevent. It's just too predictable. I want to go out with a little flair. Pizzazz!

MATTIE: I don't want you to go out at all.

LUCY: Well, with any luck then, you'll go before me and won't have to watch.

MATTIE: Oh Lucy!

LUCY: Just trying to look on the bright side.

MATTIE: Oh, I don't want any of us to end just yet. I'm not prepared. I'm not prepared for that kind of unhappiness.

LUCY: But surely that church of yours—

MATTIE: It really isn't just mine, Lucy.

LUCY: Well of course it's—

MATTIE: No it's terribly important that we understand that.

LUCY: Of course I know it's—

MATTIE: It is not just my church!!

LUCY: Why, Mattie?

MATTIE: Because it is precisely for that reason that I go. You think me shallow for needing this weekly reminder to love my neighbor, especially in this time of apparent free love. But I'm afraid I do need it Lucy... Most of the time I've the feeling of struggling along on such a lonesome journey, I can barely see beyond my own nose. But at church, I... I find I'm not alone, you see, not at all alone, but part of a much greater struggle, a struggle that's been going on for centuries, a struggle that belongs to all of us. I go to church because it broadens me, Lucy. You steer clear of the church because it would narrow you. This is a difference between you and me, and really mustn't be taken as a judgment on the church.

LUCY: I stand enlightened and humbled.

MATTIE: And whether or not this is the most direct path to understanding, it is one that I have remained on for most of my life and there must be some merit in that.

LUCY: This said to an inveterate path hopper.

MATTIE: Doesn't it confuse you? Western, Eastern, Indian, Tibetan...

LUCY: The hummingbird's tour, as Norton calls it. But I would simply rot in one place, thinking one thing. It's the exploration that keeps me alive, Mattie. This is my way of feeling a part of this struggle of yours.

MATTIE: Variety.

LUCY: Variety...

   (Pause)

MATTIE: Lucy?

LUCY: What?

MATTIE: Don't run away just yet. I'm not prepared... Stay and face it. Whatever it is... Please... Stay and face it.

   (Pause)

LUCY: I'll think on it.

MATTIE: What keeps you living where you are now? You haven't a husband, you're hardly ever there. Why don't you move in with us?

LUCY: Mattie!

MATTIE: Well, why not?

LUCY: For one thing, Norton would fly through the roof.

MATTIE: One way to get him out of the house.

LUCY: Are you serious?

MATTIE: We're good for each other. There's plenty of room.

LUCY: You are serious.

MATTIE: We could face it together. Whatever it is.

(Pause)

LUCY: It could be an unhappy ending.

MATTIE: I realize that.
(Pause)

LUCY: That is the nicest proposal I've ever received, Mattie... Thank you, I will consider the idea.
(Pause)
   What would Constance say?

(CONSTANCE pokes her head in the door)

CONSTANCE: Lucy, who do you think's going pick up your room? Moses?

(LUCY exits)

LIGHTS OUT
• END OF SCENE THREE •

ACT TWO

SCENE FOUR

LIGHTS up on CONSTANCE and NORTON. It is Easter morning. CONSTANCE stands, looking out the picture window, engrossed in something that is going on outside, and NORTON is studying the colored funny papers from the Sunday newspaper.

NORTON: Where's the rest of the paper?

CONSTANCE: Hm?

NORTON: The rest of the paper. Do you know where it is?

CONSTANCE: Most likely up in my room.

NORTON: Constance, this habit of yours is really very aggravating.

CONSTANCE: What's that?

NORTON: Squirreling away sections of the paper before I've had a chance to read them.

CONSTANCE: Hm.

NORTON: I suppose my glasses are up there too. You're not listening to a word I'm saying are you?

CONSTANCE: Now what's that damn fool think he's doing now?

NORTON: I believe it's called lawn care.

CONSTANCE: Out there messing with that mower.

NORTON: That would seem to be part of the job, wouldn't it?

CONSTANCE: Throwing around those hedge clippers like they were—

NORTON: *(Unmoved)*
No! Don't tell me he's got the hedge clippers!

CONSTANCE: Fooling around with that hose.

NORTON: *(Still with feigned annoyance)*
Let me at him!

CONSTANCE: Damned fool.

NORTON: Were you this ornery fifteen years ago?

CONSTANCE: Why?

NORTON: Well, it's a good case against aging.

CONSTANCE: Hm.

NORTON: Speaking of aging, what time did the girls say they'd be back from the home?

CONSTANCE: In time to fix us some lunch, I hope.

NORTON: I believe we say brunch today.

CONSTANCE: Brunch then.

NORTON: Some skip brunch and just say Bloody Mary.

CONSTANCE: Now, who would that be?

NORTON: Constance, let's you and me have us a little bloody together?

CONSTANCE: On Easter Sunday?

NORTON: Why not?

CONSTANCE: Makes more sense than bunnies.

(*NORTON begins to move toward the kitchen*)

NORTON: You know she's considering moving in with us?

CONSTANCE: *(Turning to him)*
Who?

NORTON: Lucy. Mattie has asked her whether she might move in. She's apparently thinking about it.

CONSTANCE: *(Smiles)*
Well I'll be.

NORTON: Constance, you're smiling.

CONSTANCE: Time she came home.

NORTON: So you think it's a peachy idea too, huh. It appears all of the women in this house have lost their senses. Mattie thinks the idea a regular humdinger.

CONSTANCE: What about you?

NORTON: Not sure what to think.

CONSTANCE: Hm mm.
> *(Smiles)*
> *(Turns back to the window)*
>> Damn fool lawn boy.

NORTON: Well. Two bloody Marys coming up!

> *(LUCY enters from the direction of the front door)*

LUCY: Make that three, would you?

NORTON: We didn't hear you come in.

LUCY: One doesn't exactly waltz through the door with renewed vigor after an experience like that.

NORTON: That bad?

LUCY: Absolutely the most dreary... The most dismal...

> *(MATTIE enters in full bunny attire, one of her ears bent)*

NORTON: There she is! What did they think of Bugs?

MATTIE: Oh I think it cheered them enormously.

LUCY: Mattie! How can you say that?!

MATTIE: The effect was subtle, I admit, but I think they had a grand time.

LUCY: Oh so that's what's meant by having a grand time. Several of them burst into tears.

MATTIE: Well that was unfortunate.

LUCY: It was altogether a fine fiasco.

MATTIE: Lucy was miserable, the women outnumbered the men nine to one.

LUCY: One of you must promise to hit me over the head with something unmistakably lethal before I ever approach such a state.

NORTON: I'd be happy to.

LUCY: Didn't you mention a Bloody Mary, Norton?

NORTON: Coming right up.

LUCY: I'll help.

MATTIE: Lucy, you're a wretched influence on Norton.

NORTON: Shall we count you in, Mattie?

MATTIE: Well, if my arm's to be twisted... Absolutely exhausted!

(*MATTIE throws herself in a chair and LUCY and NORTON exit toward the kitchen*)

CONSTANCE: returns to her post at the window)

MATTIE: Constance, what are you looking at?

CONSTANCE: Damned lawn care fool.

MATTIE: You aren't going to chase off another lawn man are you?

CONSTANCE: Out there messing around with that brand new sprinkler!

MATTIE: I'm sure he doesn't intend to harm the sprinkler. I'm afraid it's part of his job.

CONSTANCE: Hm!

MATTIE: Are you sure you're all right, Constance?

CONSTANCE: What you talking about?

MATTIE: Well you do seem a bit... testy.

CONSTANCE: No testier than I always am.

MATTIE: Come away from that window for a minute, I want to ask you something.

CONSTANCE: What's that Baby?

MATTIE: Tell me about the voices.

CONSTANCE: Now don't you worry yourself about those voices.

MATTIE: Who do you hear?

CONSTANCE: Folks who have passed away. My mother, brothers, old friends…

MATTIE: How long has this been going on?

CONSTANCE: Four or five months.

MATTIE: What do they say?

CONSTANCE: My name, generally. "Constance?" And other things.

MATTIE: They don't scare you, do they?

CONSTANCE: Why should they scare me? Just makes me think of happy times.

MATTIE: Are you happy now, Constance? If you looked back on these last years, living here with Norton and me... Would you describe them as being happy?

CONSTANCE: Have I ever said otherwise?

MATTIE: You don't weary of us do you?

CONSTANCE: What has gotten into you?

MATTIE: Oh I don't know... The rest home... all those unhappy endings... Do you truly believe in a world beyond this one? There's no doubt in your mind?

CONSTANCE: Is there in yours?

MATTIE: I'm the one who should be most convinced, you think? That church of mine. I'm afraid I'm too simple to comprehend such a place. I was a very simple child, Constance, wasn't I?

CONSTANCE: You were a sweet child.

MATTIE: I know I was considered slow.

CONSTANCE: You were a sweet child.

MATTIE: We were unattractive children, all three of us.

CONSTANCE: You don't catch me saying that.

MATTIE: Still, It must have been difficult trying to love three pale, unappealing children.

CONSTANCE: You don't hear me saying that.

MATTIE: Have we gotten any easier to love?

CONSTANCE: No. None of us has. But we've gotten a little better at loving.
(Pause as she studies Mattie)
You know, you don't have to pay me anymore.

MATTIE: You won't leave us, will you?

CONSTANCE: I'm not going anywhere until I go for good.

MATTIE: That's a relief.

CONSTANCE: And when I go, I'll be going somewhere good.

MATTE: How can you be sure, Constance?

CONSTANCE: The voices.
(Smiles to herself, and turns to Mattie)
You've never been simple, Mattie. You've been strong. The strongest one.

MATTIE: Not simple?

(NORTON and LUCY enter with Bloody Marys)

CONSTANCE: Simple. Simple was that fellow who was visiting here two weeks ago. Old what's-his-name.

LUCY: Peter?

CONSTANCE: Peter. That's it. Saint Peter. Shoowee! Now that fellow was simple. Thinking he could pull off something like that. Not with Constance around. No sirree.

NORTON: What are you saying?

CONSTANCE: Fellow waltzes in here all smiles and charm, says he'll cook everybody dinner, fixing to slip the old folks a mickey, run off with all the loot.

LUCY: Constance, you watch too much television, you sound positively paranoid.

CONSTANCE: Who are you calling paranoid? Fellow was in the paper.

NORTON: In the paper?

CONSTANCE: Today's paper. Wanted by the law.

MATTIE: Constance!

CONSTANCE: Picture of him and everything.

LUCY: Don't tell me?!

NORTON: What does it say?

CONSTANCE: Some kind of Houdini con man, by the sound of it. Butters up some poor suckers, weasels his way into their home, fixes them dinner, slips them a dumb-dumb pill and fills his pockets.

LUCY: Unbelievable!

NORTON: Quite believable.

MATTIE: Are you sure it was our boy?

CONSTANCE: With a face like that? It was him alright. I knew there was something wrong with that boy. I told him out in the kitchen I had a good mind to call the law on him.

LUCY: You said that to him?

NORTON: So he knew you were on to him. That's why he was so willing to disappear.

LUCY: This is fantastic!

    (Pause)

MATTIE: But the creature did disappear!

"Picture of him and everything"

LUCY: Yes, how can we explain that?

CONSTANCE: What do you mean?

MATTIE: Well you were here. He disappeared right before our very eyes.

CONSTANCE: Bolted, that's all.

LUCY: But we were all watching him.

MATTIE: He was standing there waving at us when suddenly—

NORTON: Constance ripped open her envelope.

CONSTANCE: That damn fool envelope.

LUCY: And we all turned to look.

MATTIE: So when we turned back—

NORTON: He'd nipped off.

CONSTANCE: Shot off like a rabbit.

MATTIE: But, Constance, you seemed just as surprised as the rest of us.

CONSTANCE: Didn't think legs like that could run that fast.

NORTON: You didn't throw away the article, did you?

CONSTANCE: Got it right upstairs.

LUCY: Well we must see it!

(CONSTANCE begins to move out of the room)

CONSTANCE: You don't want anything else from up there do you? Because this is the last time I'm climbing those stairs...

(CONSTANCE exits)

(Pause)

NORTON: Well, here stand three of the biggest boobs on record.

LUCY: What perfect idiots we've been!

NORTON: Complete hogwash, all along.

LUCY: Utter fiction!

MATTIE: Oh, I feel such a buffoon!

NORTON: Three great April fools.

LUCY: How could I have swallowed such a story?

MATTIE: Nonsense, every word.

LUCY: That horrible creature.

MATTIE: So unappealing.

LUCY: In retrospect, yes, but a brilliant disguise.

NORTON: Filled with holes, if you think about it.

LUCY: Norton, don't you dare try and rise above this.

NORTON: I'm flat on the ground with the rest of you.

LUCY: Those envelopes…

MATTIE: Oh, those awful, awful envelopes! Wicked, wicked things!

(MATTIE bursts into tears)

LUCY: What's wrong Mattie?

MATTIE: I'm almost a little disappointed.

LUCY: Disappointed?

MATTIE: Well, he seemed so ... magical.

LUCY: I didn't think you approved of magic.

MATTIE: Oh but one can long for something that one doesn't approve of. Like bourbon in the afternoon... and magical soothsayers... and, and... steamy summer romances.

NORTON: Mattie!

MATTIE: You don't think it's unseemly, do you? For a woman of my age to... well, to hope.

LUCY: Of course not.

MATTIE: I'd like to be swept off my feet. I'd like that.

LUCY: Of course you would Mattie.

MATTIE: I'm not ready to move into the home yet.

NORTON: No, no, Mattie.

MATTIE: I'm not completely washed up, am I?

LUCY: No, no, dear, no. Mattie...

(LUCY puts her arm around Mattie)

LUCY: I'm a bit disappointed too.

MATTIE: You are?

LUCY: Yes. Well, he was so kind to me. He told me things, you know.

MATTIE: What sorts of things?

LUCY: About the… the blossoming.

NORTON: Blossoming?

LUCY: He said that I would… survive.

MATTIE: Oh, Lucy.

(MATTIE holds Lucy)

NORTON: I wish someone would tell me what's going on.

MATTIE: Lucy has something.

LUCY: There is a small mystery about my mid-section.

NORTON: What sort of mystery?

LUCY: A small… mass, of some sort.

NORTON: Lucy.

LUCY: Nothing conclusive, just vexing.

NORTON: I had no idea.

LUCY: And Peter… or whomever it was I invested with my pathetic, flip-flopping faith… The point is he promised…

(LUCY covers her mouth and burst into tears)

MATTIE: Oh, poor Lucy.

NORTON: Of course you will survive this Lucy.

LUCY: You think so?

NORTON: We will see that you survive. We will see that you get the right help. We will see to it.

LUCY: Thank you Norton.

NORTON: You don't need some wigged-out wizard to tell you whether or not you will survive.

LUCY: Thank you.

NORTON: We will see to it. And, we will have no more illness. No more death. No more people being taken too soon. We'll have no more of it! No more sadness!
(NORTON bursts into tears)
(The TWO SISTERS watch, afraid to move in for a hug)

(Pause)

MATTIE: Norton?

NORTON: The man did say something to me, in the kitchen.

LUCY: Yes?

NORTON: I found it comforting.

MATTIE: What was it?

NORTON: That love… the sort of love that I had for Cynthia, the sort that she had for me… that this out-pouring of love, for the other, would never deplete us, either of us. That the more we poured… the more we were filled, and that this fullness was…

LUCY: Yes?

NORTON: Eternal.

MATTIE: Oh, Norton.

LUCY: Dear, dear.
    (ALL THREE gather for a group hug and cry)

(CONSTANCE enters)

CONSTANCE: Good night-a'mighty!

    (The THREE SIBLINGS turn to look at Constance)

CONSTANCE: They just dropped the bomb?!

MATTIE: No Constance. We're just having a nice hug.

CONSTANCE: Liked to scare me to death. Three old uptight WASPS hanging all over each other.

    (MATTIE runs over and hugs Constance)

MATTIE: Constance you must promise to live forever.

CONSTANCE: What has gotten into you?

LUCY: You may not realize it, Constance, but you have just risen from the dead.

CONSTANCE: Well, alleluia.

MATTIE: There's one question still unanswered.

NORTON: What's that?

MATTIE: Who was it peeked?

LUCY: Peeked?

MATTIE: In the envelopes.

NORTON: Yes. The prize sap of us all.

CONSTANCE: You mean the ones that fellow wrote out for you?

LUCY: Don't tell me it was you, Constance.

CONSTANCE: Wanted to see did he have anybody's birthday right.

MATTIE: Well this is all too humorous. We've been so ill behaved!

LUCY: Is that the article? Let's see.

> *(CONSTANCE hands a folded section of the paper to Lucy)*

MATTIE: Let's have a look.

(THE THREE SIBLINGS move over to the window and all look at the paper which is held at arm's length, down and flat, to catch the light from the window and because they are all farsighted)
(CONSTANCE joins them at the window for a moment)

CONSTANCE: Damn fool lawn boy.

(CONSTANCE moves out of the room)

(ALL THREE stand squinting at the article)

NORTON: I can't tell, do you think it looks like our man?

LUCY: I don't have my glasses.

MATTIE: It's not a wonderful likeness. Norton, do you have a pair of glasses?

NORTON: I can never keep a pair of glasses with Constance around.

LUCY: Well it's very close, certainly.

MATTIE: Can you see, Lucy?

LUCY: No, not a bit. Can't see a thing without my glasses.

NORTON: Face looks a bit fleshy, but I can't begin to see it.

LUCY: A photo will add some pounds, they say.

MATTIE: When one is fleshy, one photographs fleshy.

NORTON: Fleshy?

MATTIE: You didn't find him fleshy?

NORTON: Are we talking about the same person?

LUCY: I wish I could see his eyes, no mistaking those eyes.

MATTIE: Well, I did my best to avoid them.

LUCY: Oh Mattie that's too funny.

NORTON: Now girls. We were all duped.

LUCY: Mattie your glasses are on top of your head.

MATTIE: Oh, for goodness sakes.

(MATTIE *puts on her glasses, takes the newspaper and gasps*)

LUCY: What? What do you see?
(LUCY *takes the glasses off of Mattie's face and looks at the paper. LUCY gasps*)

NORTON: What? What?

(NORTON *grabs the glasses from Lucy and gasps*)

MATTIE: Nothing like him!

LUCY: Nothing.

NORTON: The lawn man could pass for him better than this guy!

(NORTON *tosses the newspaper aside*)

(ALL THREE *look out the window*)

NORTON: What is Constance doing out there?

MATTIE: Don't tell me she's worrying the poor man.

NORTON: That's exactly what she's doing.

MATTIE: Why does she insist on driving these people away?

NORTON: They don't grow on trees, that's a fact.

LUCY: Well, you're certainly lucky to have landed this one.

MATTIE: Why do you say that?

LUCY: I could never get someone out where I live on Easter Sunday.

(Pause, ALL THREE stare out the window Mysterious MUSIC slowly rises as LIGHTS begin to swirl around in front of them. THEY stare out the window, stunned)

MATTIE: Look.

NORTON: Damndest thing.

LUCY: Constance.

MATTIE: That smile.

LUCY: That smile.

MATTIE: Highly uncharacteristic.

NORTON: Damndest thing.

LUCY: Looks positively demented.

NORTON: Damndest thing.

MATTIE: What, Norton?

NORTON: Her feet.

MATTIE: Her feet?

LUCY: Her feet.

MATTIE: They don't appear to be...

LUCY: To be...

MATTIE: They don't appear to be touching...

LUCY: To be touching the...

MATTIE: They don't appear to be touching the...

NORTON: Damndest thing...

> *(In unison, ALL THREE slowly begin to move their eyes up into the sky as if Constance is rising from the earth. THEY press their heads in closer and closer toward the glass, finally having to bend over*

and twist their heads sideways to follow her journey up into the clouds. LIGHTS and SOUND rise and rise. When THEY can no longer see her, THEY straighten, and return to their upright positions looking directly out the window. The MUSIC stops and LIGHTS return to normal)
(Long pause, as THE SIBLINGS stare out the window. Stunned)

(NORTON dashes out the door)

(MATTIE and LUCY continue to stand looking out the window with a look of shock on their faces.

(THEY finally turn to each other and stare some more)

MATTIE: What must the lawn man think?!

(The WOMEN look back out at the lawn man, THEY cover their mouths— uncover their mouths)

MATTIE & LUCY: Peter!!

(MATTIE and LUCY again turn to one another, then slowly turn back to look out the window)

(Suddenly the WOMEN screech, grab each other and register utter shock)

(Long pause)

MATTIE: Poof.

LUCY: Poof.

MATTIE: Poof.

LUCY: Poof.

(NORTON runs back in, leans over to catch his breath, straightens up)

NORTON: Poof.

(NORTON bends over, holding his knees some more and tries to regain his breath)

(Pause)

NORTON: No life. In her body. No life…
   (Pause)
     What we saw was the…

MATTIE & LUCY: Spirit?

NORTON: As it…

(NORTON waves his hand around)

(MATTIE and LUCY wave their hands around, flapping and indicating that the spirit rose up in the sky)

(Silence)

NORTON: I'll go and phone the police.

(NORTON exits toward the kitchen)
(MATTIE and LUCY look out with blank stares, stunned)

LUCY: Do you think we'll recognize him when he comes for us?

MATTIE: Doubtful.

LUCY: Perhaps that's a blessing.

(Pause)

MATTIE: I wish I'd been braver.

LUCY: Braver?

MATTIE: If I'd been able to look him in the eyes, I might have seen something… something genuine. If only we'd been kinder to him.

LUCY: Well, I suppose he's used to that.

MATTIE: We might have been kinder to you about him.

LUCY: Oh that's to be expected. I've been known to exaggerate.

MATTIE: Mm... Still... I hope we'll be more generous next time.
(Pause)
I have a little confession to make... I prayed that Constance might leave soon.

LUCY: Of course you did, Mattie, she was exhausted.

MATTIE: She was... Old Mrs. Doom.

(MATTIE and LUCY smile and wipe their eyes)

(NORTON enters)

NORTON: They're on their way. Should be here in a few minutes.

(Pause as they look out the window)

(LUCY finally moves over and picks up the envelopes SHE gives one to Mattie and one to Norton, keeping her own)

LUCY: There are some things that we really weren't meant to know.

(LUCY rips her envelope in half)

MATTIE: It still has to be lived, doesn't it?

NORTON: What?

MATTIE: Life.
(SHE rips her envelope in half)
It's life that has to be lived. Life. Whether it's in this room, or in the garden. Whether it's in the old age home, or in the next world, it has to be lived.

(MATTIE tears her envelope in tiny pieces)

LUCY: Whether the thing happens tomorrow, in three years or twenty, it has to be lived.

(LUCY rips her envelope into tiny pieces)
(NORTON hesitates)

LUCY: Norton?

NORTON: I'd like to know… I was hoping to know when I might see her.

LUCY: Of course.

NORTON: But, I suppose I need to figure on some reason for my being here.
(HE rips his envelope into tiny pieces)
(Pause)
I think I'd like to start walking again.

MATTIE: Really?

NORTON: Cynthia used to tell me that no one ever got to the end of a walk and said, "I wish I hadn't taken that walk."

MATTIE: I'd like to join you.

LUCY: You should, Mattie. Get out among the ambulatory. I, on the other hand, would like to sit still for a while. Maybe read something of the professor's.

NORTON: So you'll stay, Lucy?

LUCY: Do you think I should?

NORTON: Constance smiled, you know, when I told her you might be staying. She smiled.

LUCY: Then I suppose I must stay. Thank you.

MATTIE: To Constance.

NORTON & LUCY: To Constance.

(ALL THREE SIBLINGS toss their envelope confetti in the air)

(A SNOW BAG releases tiny bits of paper from the sky)

(LIGHTS fade with the confetti raining overhead)

THE END

www.ingramcontent.com/pod-product-compliance
Lightning Source LLC
Chambersburg PA
CBHW030438010526
44118CB00011B/690